Lukas FOSS

ELEGY
for Clarinet and Piano

Edited by Richard Stoltzman

Piano

Rental materials for Clarinet and Orchestra
available exclusively from Keiser Classical:

1-855-259-6495 Toll-free (U.S./Canada)
rental@laurenkeisermusic.com

KEISER
CLASSICAL

Elegy for Clarinet and Orchestra – 1949 Lukas Foss

The life of Lukas Foss brimmed with a heady mix of music, art, intellectual electricity and a sustained sense of wonder, curiosity, and virtuosity. He was brilliant in everything—always challenging the status quo.

We formed a friendship which delighted us and many audiences, performing composers with whom he had intimate and illustrious relationships such as Bernstein, Copland, and Hindemith. Lukas could regale us with personal anecdotes, and artistic insights from a deep connection with essential music of the entire 20th century.

He allowed me to arrange his *Three American Pieces*, originally violin and piano, for clarinet. He composed a chamber work for the TASHI group and then refashioned it as a magical concerto for clarinet and orchestra. Then one day, he simply presented me with this manuscript *Elegy for Clarinet and Orchestra - 1949* saying, "I found this among some stacks of my music. It's never been played and there are no orchestral parts, just this score. Maybe you'll play it someday."

After Lukas died, I told his wife and son, Christopher, about this gift and we decided we must bring it into the world. The orchestration calls for timpani, cymbal, gong, tom tom, triangle and bass drum. The tempo mark, Andante ♩ = 58, provides the somber procession that Lukas asks the clarinet for "cantabile" (singing), "espressivo," "dolce" (sweetly), "grazioso" (gracefully). A clarinet cadenza suggests the dual meaning of elegy—lament and praise.

Richard Stoltzman

Edited by Richard Stoltzman

to Artie Shaw

ELEGY
for Clarinet in B♭ and Orchestra

LUKAS FOSS
(1949)

* The right hand taps the low strings beyond the damper pedal, simulating cymbals, bass drum and gong (*pp*).

4

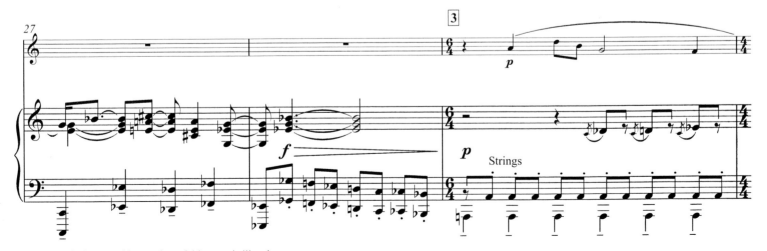

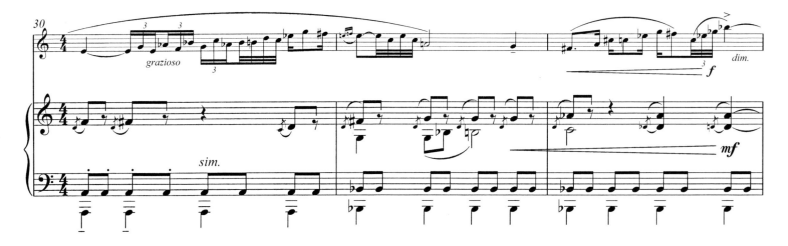

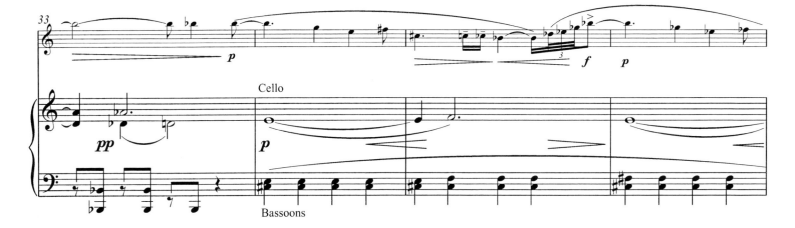

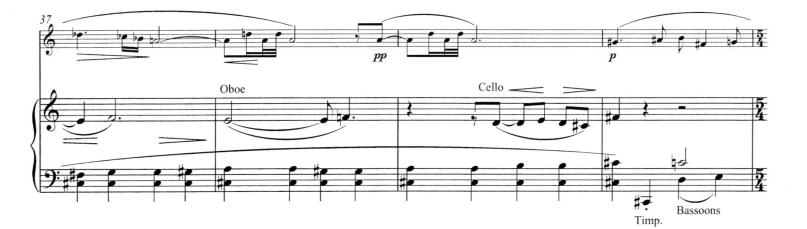

6

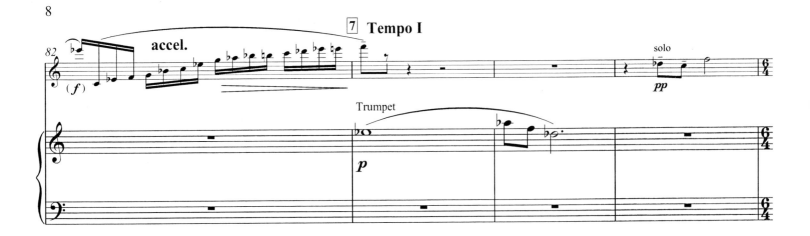

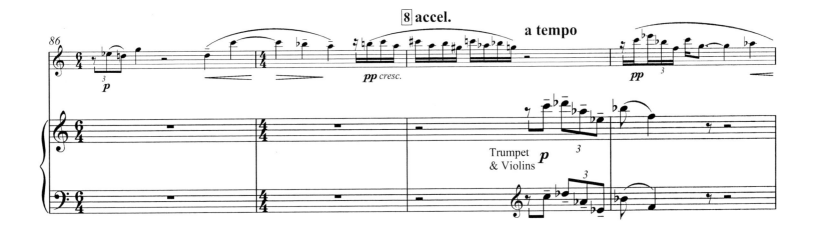

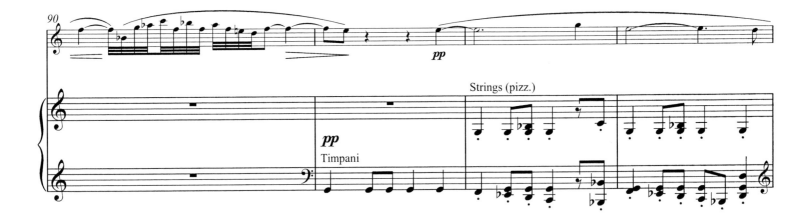

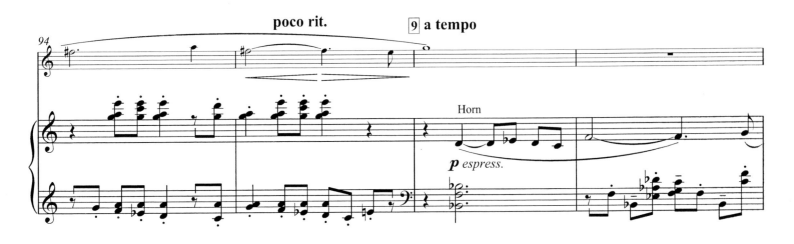

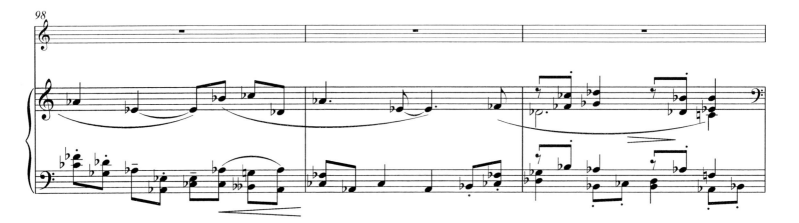

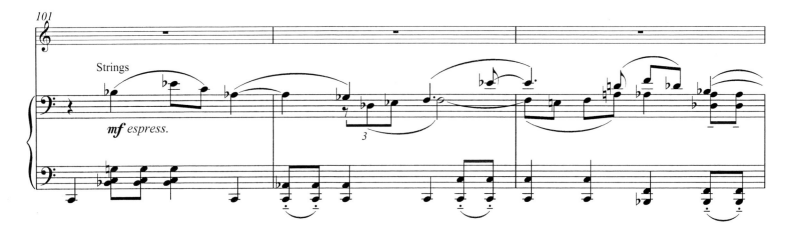

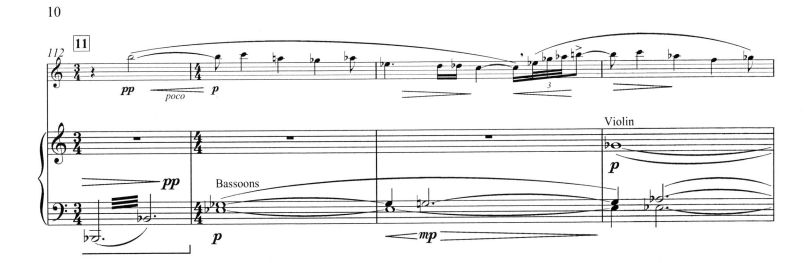

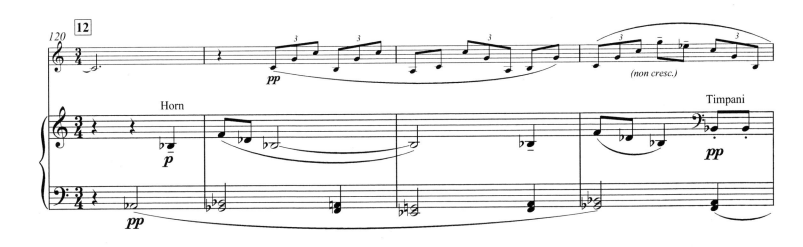

Richard Stoltzman
21st Century Series for Clarinet

Richard Stoltzman's virtuosity, musicianship and sheer personal magnetism have made him one of today's most sought-after concert artists. As soloist with more than a hundred orchestras, as a captivating recitalist and chamber music performer, as an innovative jazz artist, and as a prolific recording artist, two-time Grammy Award winner Stoltzman has defied categorization, dazzling critics and audiences alike throughout many musical genres.

"His mastery of the clarinet and his impeccable musicianship are no secret by now, but one who has not heard him play for a time can easily forget how rich and fluid the instrument can sound from top to bottom of its range. If Mr. Stoltzman is not one of a kind, who might the others be?" - The New York Times

SCHUBERT SONATINES 1 & 2, OPUS 137 FOR CLARINET AND PIANO WITH CD Stoltzman, called the "greatest clarinetist in the world" by the Boston Globe, has transcribed and edited two Schubert Sonatines originally written for Violin, Op. posth. 137 for the clarinet. These two brilliant Sonatines, No. 1 in D (D384) and No. 2 in a minor (D385) are expertly engraved, formatted and set in a lovely edition with high quality paper. Both Sonatines are available in one folio. Sonatine No. 1 is transcribed for Clarinet in A and No. 2 for Bb Clarinet. Mr. Stoltzman provides insights and performance suggestions in this classic edition.
HLC00042593.. $22.95

BACH CHROMATIC FANTASIA AND FUGUE IN D MINOR WITH CD This masterly and sublime classic J. S. Bach work has been expertly transcribed and arranged for three clarinets that begins with a solo clarinet tour de force edited by world class artist Richard Stoltzman. The CD recording provides performance insights to the Fantasia and accompaniment for the Fugue. Now clarinetists can play this masterwork in a setting created by one of the world's greatest clarinet players. This edition encompasses expert music engraving and quality paper and printing. It should be in every clarinet player's library for a lifetime of enjoyment and admiration.
HLC00042681 .... $19.95

BRAHMS INTERMEZZO OP. 118, NO. 2 In the span of three years, Brahms composed a veritable treasure trove of clarinet music. First came the Trio, Op. 114, which was followed in the same year by the Quintet, Op. 115 (1891). Then, in 1894 he gave us his Sonatas: Op. 120 No. 1 &2. Nestled amidst these fervid works is the melancholy Intermezzo, Op. 118 No. 2 (1893). Though written for the piano, one can easily imagine the memory of Richard Mühlfeld, Brahms' "nightingale" of the clarinet, haunting the melodic lines which seem to flow so effortlessly. In this transcription of Brahms' Intermezzo from his "Six Pieces for Piano", Op. 118,. the clarinetist may choose to perform in the original key of A, with parts provided for A and B-flat clarinets; or in an alternate version in B-flat (includes transposed piano score and B-flat clarinet part).
HLC00046282 .... $10.95

HARTKE CONCERTO FOR CLARINET- "LANDSCAPES WITH BLUES" Written for the IRIS Chamber Orchestra's inaugural season, Stephen Hartke's work reflects on the old time blues heritage of the Mississippi Delta. This new edition offers for the first time a clarinet solo part edited with commentary by internationally-acclaimed clarinet artist Richard Stoltzman. Includes piano reduction by Sarah Gibson along with a CD containing Stoltzman's original recording with the IRIS Chamber Orchestra.
HLC00127805... $39.95

FOSS ELEGY FOR CLARINET AND PIANO Lukas Foss was asked by Artie Shaw in the 1940s for a new work. Foss composed "Elegy" for clarinet and orchestra. The manuscript was given to Richard Stoltzman by Foss just before his death. Foss and Stoltzman concertized together for many years but never played this work. Stoltzman edited this beautiful work and presented the world premiere transcription for clarinet and piano in 2014. We are honored to publish this Foss gem in Richard's Stoltzman's series for clarinet.
HLC00144421... $19.95

Products and Ordering
www.halleonard.com

Questions or comments?
info@laurenkeisermusic.com

Prices and availability of all items subject to change.

PUBLICATIONS FOR CLARINET FROM SOUTHERN MUSIC

METHODS
Edited by DAVID HITE

Artistic Studies Bk. 1 from the FRENCH School   B362
40 Studies and 32 Etudes by Cyrill Rose (1830-1903).
All of the classic Rose studies in one volume.

Artistic Studies Bk. 2 from the GERMAN School   B367
Carl Baermann Method: Part IV (selected) and Part V (complete).
Indispensable virtuoso studies for the clarinet.

Artistic Studies Bk. 3 from the ITALIAN School   B390
The best of the Italian operatic-oriented virtuoso studies including the
work of Cavallini, Lebanchi, Magnani, and Gambaro.

Baermann Foundation Studies for Clarinet   B398
An expanded version of the famous Baermann, Part III
method devoted to scales, intervals and chords in all keys.

Melodious and Progressive Studies, Book I   B448
Demnitz: 36 Expressive Studies; Nocentini: 24 Melodic Studies;
Baermann: 24 Melodic Etudes with major and minor scales in thirds.
For study after completion of any beginning clarinet method.

Melodious and Progressive Studies, Book II   B451
Gambaro: 20 Caprices; Dont: 20 Etudes with other special studies.
Valuable as a bridge into the advanced level.

DUETS
Edited by DAVID HITE

Forty Progressive Melodies (Barrett) B382
Seven Grand Concert Duets B521
Includes works by Haydn, Mozart, Crusell and Klose

Three Artistic Duets (Cavallini) B538
Six Grand Duets (Cavallini) B539

SOLO REPERTOIRE
with piano accompaniment

LEVEL II
ST790 Minuet and Allegro .... J.C. BACH-Voxman
SS713 Introduction and Rondo .... DIABELLI-Hite
SS93 Piece in g minor ....Gabriel PIERNE
SU1 Sicilienne .... PARADIS-Hite
SS158 Etude .... RABAUD-Hite
SS76 Wessex Pastorale.......................................STOCKS-Bonade

LEVEL III
SS710 Bouree .... BACH-Hite
ST986 Adagio.. BAERMANN-Hite
SS712 Adagio and Gigue ....CORELLI-Hite
ST727 La Fille Au Cheveux de lin ....DEBUSSY-Hite
ST708 Petite Piece ....DEBUSSY-Hite
SS274 Andante de Concert...........................FERLING-JeanJean
SS277 Rigaudon.....................................LACOME-Andraud
SS718 Larghetto from Quintet .... MOZART-Hite

LEVEL IV
ST638 Divertimento ....BAERMANN-Forrest
SS717 Andante and Scherzo...DERE-Hite
SS92 Canzonetta..Gabriel PIERNE
SS281 Petite Piece ....L. QUET
SS97 Sonata in g minor .... TARTINI-Hite

LEVEL V
ST848 Adagio and Tarantella ....CAVALLINI-Hite
SS276 Fantaisie.....................................Augusta HOLMES
SS282 Solo de Concours...................................... Henri RABAUD
16 Grands Solos de Concert.. D. BONADE

LEVEL VI
ST860 Sonata ....Samuel ADLER
ST909 Intrigues (with band) ....Andreas MAKRIS
ST707 Premiere Rhapsodie.....................................DEBUSSY-Hite
ST726 Concerto No.3, Op. 11................................CRUSELL-Hite

Southern MUSIC
Exclusively Distributed By
HAL•LEONARD CORPORATION